River Patrol Boats

by Michael Green

Consultant:
Kerry N. Schaefer, President
PBR Forces Veterans Association, Inc.

CAPSTONE
HIGH/LOW BOOKS
an imprint of Capstone Press
Mankato, Minnesota

Capstone High/Low Books are published by Capstone Press
818 North Willow Street • Mankato, MN 56001
http://www.capstone-press.com

Library of Congress Cataloging-in-Publication Data
Green, Michael, 1952-
    River patrol boats/by Michael Green.
        p. cm. — (Land and sea)
    Includes bibliographical references and index.
    Summary: Briefly describes the development, weapons, and use of
river patrol boats from the Revolutionary War days through the Vietnam
War.
    ISBN 0-7368-0043-3
    1. Vedette boats—Juvenile literature. 2. Riverine operations—United
States—Juvenile literature. [1. Gunboats. 2. Riverine operations.] I. Title.
II. Series: Land and sea (Mankato, Minn.)
V880.G744 1999
359.8'358'0973—dc21

                                                              98-15240
                                                                  CIP
                                                                  AC

Editorial credits
Matt Doeden, editor; James Franklin, cover designer and illustrator;
    Sheri Gosewisch, photo researcher

Photo credits
Department of Defense, 36
Michael Green, 14, 29, 43
National Archives, 19
U.S. Naval Historical Center, 30, 35
U.S. Navy, cover, 4, 7, 8, 11, 13, 16, 21, 22, 24, 32, 38, 41

Table of Contents

Chapter 1

River Patrol Boats

Many people think of large warships when they think of the U.S. Navy. But some of the navy's most important watercraft have been shallow-water boats. The navy once had an entire fleet of shallow-water boats. A fleet is a group of watercraft under one command.

The navy called its fleet of shallow-water boats the Brown Water Navy. This is because shallow water is muddy and often appears brown. The navy called its fleet of large ships the Blue Water Navy. This is because deep water usually appears blue.

The U.S. Navy once had a fleet of shallow-water boats.

The Brown Water Navy included riverine boats. Riverine boats could enter rivers from oceans. They could patrol rivers.

The navy used riverine boats for many years. Riverine boats were used most during the Vietnam War (1954–1975).

Tasks

During the Vietnam War, the navy used riverine boats to patrol rivers and other shallow waters. Crews searched for enemy boats. This was difficult. Enemy boats often looked much like the boats of fishers and other Vietnamese people. Crew members stopped and searched the boats they thought carried enemy weapons and supplies.

Riverine boat crew members reported any enemy boats they found to naval leaders. They sometimes followed the enemy boats. Other times they destroyed the boats.

Size and Speed

Riverine boats were small. Most were from 30 to 60 feet (nine to 18 meters) long. They

Riverine boats were small.

weighed from seven to 60 tons (six to 54
metric tons).

People measure the speed of ships and
boats in knots. One knot equals 1.15 miles
(1.85 kilometers) per hour. Riverine boats
traveled at speeds between eight and 40 knots.

The speed of riverine boats depended mostly on their weight.

Their speed depended mostly on their weight. Riverine boats that had armor were slower than those that did not. Armor is a protective metal covering.

Weapons and Armor

Riverine boats carried guns, cannons, and
grenades to attack enemies. Crew members
did not need large guns or explosives to
destroy other riverine boats. Small guns
usually were enough to destroy enemy boats.

Riverine boat crew members used grenades to destroy large enemy targets. They usually launched these small explosives with grenade launchers. These weapons shoot grenades long distances. Grenade launchers allowed crew members to attack enemies from safe distances.

Some riverine boats carried flame throwers. A flame thrower is a weapon that shoots out flames. Crew members used flame throwers to burn away plants that could hide enemies.

Few riverine boats had armor. Armor protected the boats from enemy fire. But the armor also slowed down the boats. Slow boats were easier for enemies to attack than fast boats.

Crews

Riverine boats had crews of at least four people. Many boats had larger crews. Every

Crew members used grenade launchers to destroy large enemy targets.

riverine boat crew contained one boat captain, one gunner's mate, and one engineman. The crew usually contained a patrol officer too.

Each crew member had a job. The boat captain was in charge of the boat. He made all of the important decisions on the boat. The gunner's mate operated the boat's weapons. He also fixed weapons when they broke down. The engineman maintained all the boat's engines and pumps. The patrol officer was in charge of the mission. A mission is a military task. The patrol officer kept in contact with navy bases.

Most riverine boats carried additional crew members. The extra members often were low-ranking sailors. These members helped with tasks such as cleaning and operating weapons. They also performed more important jobs as needed.

A gunner's mate operated a riverine boat's weapons.

Radar

Radio Antenna

Machine Gun

Hull

Life Preserver

Search Light

Machine Gun

Guard Rail

Patrol Boat, River

Chapter 2

Early History

The U.S. Navy began using riverine boats during the early 1800s. It used riverine boats in many major wars. The navy also used the boats to defeat pirates during the early 1820s.

The navy stopped using riverine boats several times during its early history. But it always found another use for them.

Early Uses

The U.S. Navy used riverine boats in the War of 1812 (1812–1815). Great Britain attacked the United States from Canada during the war. British ships sailed across Lake Erie. The U.S. Navy fought the British ships with small

The U.S. Navy has used riverine boats in many major wars.

shallow-water boats. Shallow-water boats helped the U.S. military patrol rivers during the war. The patrols made it difficult for the British military to move troops and supplies.

The navy used its shallow-water boats to fight pirates during the early 1820s. Pirates attacked ships on the Caribbean Sea. The pirates stole the ships' supplies and often killed the people on board. Crews aboard the navy's shallow-water boats captured and destroyed many pirate ships. The crews helped make the Caribbean Sea safer for other ships.

The Civil War

In 1861, the Civil War (1861-1865) broke out between the Northern and Southern states. The Southern states formed a separate country called the Confederate States of America. But the Northern states wanted to keep all the states as one country. The group of Northern states called itself the Union.

Riverine boats helped the Union win the Civil War. Crews patrolled major rivers along

Riverine boats helped the Union win the Civil War.

battle lines. They blocked the Confederate states from receiving supplies by ship. The crews did not let Confederate troops cross rivers. This reduced the number of Confederate troops that could reach battles.

World War II

The navy had little need for shallow-water boats after the Civil War. It did not use them again until World War II (1939–1945). The U.S. Navy and its allies fought Japan on the Pacific Ocean during World War II.

The Japanese military used ships called barges to carry supplies from island to island. The barges traveled mainly across shallow waters. Large U.S. warships could not reach the barges. Navy leaders needed small boats to reach and destroy the barges.

The navy had a fleet of small patrol torpedo (PT) boats. The PT boats could serve as shallow-water boats. PT boats used torpedoes to destroy enemy warships. A torpedo is an explosive that travels underwater. The navy replaced some PT boats' torpedoes with large guns and rockets. It sent PT boats into shallow waters to find and destroy Japanese barges. PT boats

The U.S. Navy used PT boats as shallow-water boats during World War II.

destroyed many Japanese weapons and supplies this way. This helped the United States and its allies win the war.

After World War II

Many U.S. leaders believed the navy did not need shallow-water boats after World War II.

The U.S. Navy's greatest need for riverine boats came during the Vietnam War.

They believed the United States needed only its Blue Water Navy. The navy scrapped many of its small boats when the war ended.

Navy leaders did not realize they still
needed shallow-water boats until the early
1960s. The U.S. military became heavily
involved in the Vietnam War at that time.

Chapter 3

The Vietnam War

The U.S. military fought alongside the South Vietnamese military during the Vietnam War. These two forces fought against the North Vietnamese military. Both sides wanted all of Vietnam to be one country. But each side wanted the country to have a different kind of government.

The United States sent many troops and equipment to Vietnam for the war. The navy used more riverine boats during the Vietnam War than during any other war. But the United States and South Vietnam could not defeat the North Vietnamese military.

The U.S. Navy used more riverine boats during the Vietnam War than during any other war.

Vietnam's Shallow Waters

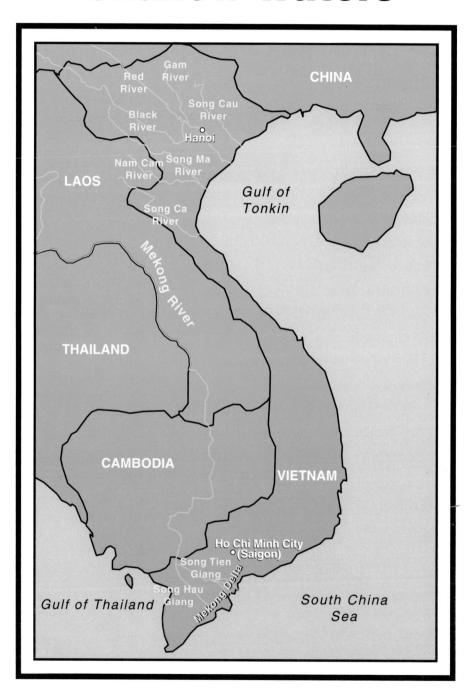

Vietnam's Shallow Waters

Vietnam is a long, narrow country. Water forms its entire eastern border. The Gulf of Tonkin lies along its northeast coast. The Gulf of Thailand lies along its southwest tip. The South China Sea borders Vietnam's east coast.

Many rivers flow through Vietnam. The main rivers are the Mekong River and the Red River. The Mekong River is the largest river in Asia.

Many riverine boats patrolled the Mekong Delta. The Mekong River enters the South China Sea in this area. Nine small rivers called the Nine Dragons flow out of the Mekong River to form this delta.

During the Vietnam War, the Vietnamese people relied on the country's rivers for much of their transportation. Vietnam did not have good roads. Both the North Vietnamese military and the South Vietnamese military used rivers to move weapons and supplies.

Few ships of the Blue Water Navy could travel along Vietnam's rivers. But small craft such as riverine boats could travel on these waters easily.

PBRs

The Patrol Boat, River (PBR) was the navy's most common riverine boat during the Vietnam War. These boats were about 31 feet (nine meters) long. They weighed only seven tons (six metric tons). The fastest PBRs could travel up to 40 knots.

The navy used a strong, light material called fiberglass in PBR hulls. A hull is the main body of a ship or boat. Fiberglass hulls made PBRs easy to move on water. Crew members could take PBRs into water as shallow as 18 inches (46 centimeters).

There were two kinds of PBRs. The first PBRs were part of the Mark I class. These boats had problems. River plants clogged up their water pumps easily. Many of their parts

PBRs were the U.S. Navy's most common riverine boats.

wore out quickly. So the navy built an improved
class of PBRs called the Mark II. Mark II PBRs
had fewer problems than Mark I PBRs. They
were slightly larger than Mark I PBRs. They also
had more powerful engines.

The U.S. Navy used mine sweeping boats to search for mines.

MSBs

The North Vietnamese military planted mines on many of the waterways the U.S. Navy patrolled. A mine is a device that explodes when another object applies pressure to it. The

U.S. Navy built mine sweeping boats (MSBs) to search for these mines.

A single mine could destroy an entire riverine boat. It could kill all the crew members. Crew members on MSBs found

Monitors such as this one protected Armored Troop Carriers.

mines and detonated them safely. Detonate
means to make an explosive blow up.

ATCs and Monitors
The navy used landing craft from World War II
as riverine troop carriers in Vietnam. Landing

craft transport supplies from sea to land. The navy used boats called Landing Craft, Medium (LCM). These World War II craft could carry 120 troops. They worked well in shallow water. But they had no armor.

The navy rebuilt the LCMs with armor. The navy called them Armored Troop Carriers (ATCs). Armor made ATCs slow. They traveled at about six knots. But armor also made the boats safer from enemy fire.

The navy built another kind of riverine boat to protect ATCs. It called these boats monitors. The navy gave monitors powerful weapons such as guns and howitzers. A howitzer is a cannon that shoots explosive shells long distances. Some monitors also carried flame throwers.

Base Ships

Crews needed places to dock their riverine boats during the Vietnam War. They needed to dock their boats away from land to keep them safe. The navy used a ship called the Landing Ship, Dock (LSD) as a riverine boat base. During World War II, the navy used LSDs to carry small amphibious craft. Amphibious means able to work on land or water. LSDs served as good base ships for small riverine boats.

The navy also used the Landing Ship, Tank (LST) as a riverine boat base. During World War II, the navy used LSTs to carry tanks to land. Later, these ships served as good bases for large riverine boats.

Helicopter Support

The navy's riverine forces relied on helicopters during the Vietnam War. Helicopters flew ahead of riverine boats to scout for enemies. Some helicopters carried wounded crew members to safety.

The U.S. Navy used LSTs as riverine boat bases.

The U.S. Navy provided helicopter support with helicopters such as this Sea Stallion.

The U.S. Army provided most of the helicopter support for riverine boats. The army used the UH-1B Iroquois helicopter for these missions.

The navy also provided some helicopter support. Navy helicopters included the UH-34 Seahorse, the CH-46 Sea Knight, and the CH-53 Sea Stallion.

Chapter 4

Riverine Boats Today

The U.S. Navy has little need for a force of riverine boats today. It keeps some riverine boats to train navy members. But the navy has not needed the boats for a war since the 1970s.

Riverine Boats after Vietnam

The navy gave most of its riverine boats to the South Vietnamese military during the early 1970s. The U.S. military left the boats behind when the United States pulled out of the Vietnam War. Navy leaders hoped the South Vietnamese military could use the boats. The

The U.S. Navy has not needed riverine boats since the 1970s.

U.S. government still wanted South Vietnam to win the war.

The South Vietnamese military could not hold off the North Vietnamese military without U.S. assistance. Few South Vietnamese soldiers had proper training to operate the riverine boats. South Vietnam also ran out of fuel for the boats.

The North Vietnamese military defeated South Vietnam in 1975. North Vietnam captured all of the remaining riverine boats. The navy does not know what happened to most of the boats after the war.

Modern Shallow-Water Boats

Today, the navy uses some patrol coastal (PC) boats. PC boats are shallow-water boats that patrol coastlines. PC boats are larger than riverine boats. They are about 170 feet (52 meters) long. They weigh more than 300 tons (272 metric tons).

Today, the navy uses patrol coastal boats to patrol shallow coastlines.

The navy still uses mine sweeping boats (MSBs). Modern MSBs are larger than those used during the Vietnam War. These boats search for mines near coastlines instead of on rivers.

The Navy has only a few PBRs left. It uses them to train special units such as SEALs. SEAL stands for Sea, Air, and Land. The Navy SEALs is a specially trained combat group within the navy.

Restored Boats

Some groups restore riverine boats from the Vietnam War to their original condition. These groups search for remaining riverine boats. The boats they find often have missing parts. Others have parts that are in bad shape. The groups replace these parts. They try to make the boats look just as they did during the Vietnam War.

Some naval museums display restored riverine boats. These museums give visitors a chance to see a part of naval history.

The navy uses its remaining PBRs to train special units.

Words to Know

armor (AR-mur)—a protective metal covering

delta (DEL-tuh)—an area where a river enters the sea

fiberglass (FYE-bur-glass)—a strong, light material

fleet (FLEET)—a group of ships under one command

grenade (gruh-NADE)—a small explosive

howitzer (HOU-uht-sur)—a cannon that shoots explosive shells long distances

hull (HUHL)—the main body of a ship or boat

knot (NOT)—a measurement of speed for ships; one knot equals 1.15 miles (1.85 kilometers) per hour.

mine (MINE)—a device that explodes when another object applies pressure to it

restore (ri-STOR)—to bring back to an original condition

riverine (riv-ur-EEN)—having to do with rivers

torpedo (tor-PEE-doh)—an explosive that travels underwater

To Learn More

Dahl, Michael. *Vietnam.* Countries of the World. Mankato, Minn.: Bridgestone Books, 1998.

Gay, Kathlyn and Martin Gay. *Vietnam War.* Voices from the Past. New York: Twenty-First Century Books, 1996.

Green, Michael. *PT Boats.* Land and Sea. Mankato, Minn.: Capstone High/Low Books, 1999.

Green, Michael. *The United States Navy.* Serving Your Country. Mankato, Minn.: Capstone High/Low Books, 1998.

Useful Addresses

Naval Historical Center
Washington Navy Yard
901 M Street SE
Washington, DC 20374-5060

Navy Public Affairs Office
Naval Sea Systems Command
Washington, DC 20362

PBR Forces Veterans Association, Inc.
732 American Inn Road
Villa Ridge, MO 63089-2214

Internet Sites

The Mobile Riverine Force Association Home Page
http://www.mrfa.org

Naval Historical Center
http://www.history.navy.mil

PBR Forces Veterans Association, Inc.
http://www.pbr-fva.org

U.S. Navy: Welcome Aboard
http://www.navy.mil

Index